Communism in Our World

By John C. Caldwell

LET'S VISIT ARGENTINA

LET'S VISIT AMERICANS OVERSEAS

LET'S VISIT BRAZIL

LET'S VISIT CEYLON

LET'S VISIT CHINA

LET'S VISIT COLOMBIA

LET'S VISIT FORMOSA

LET'S VISIT INDIA

LET'S VISIT INDONESIA

LET'S VISIT JAPAN

LET'S VISIT KOREA (WITH ELSIE F. CALDWELL)

LET'S VISIT MIDDLE AFRICA

LET'S VISIT THE MIDDLE EAST

LET'S VISIT PAKISTAN

LET'S VISIT PERU

LET'S VISIT THE PHILIPPINES

LET'S VISIT SOUTHEAST ASIA

LET'S VISIT WEST AFRICA

LET'S VISIT THE WEST INDIES

By John C. Caldwell and Elsie F. Caldwell

OUR NEIGHBORS IN AFRICA

OUR NEIGHBORS IN INDIA

OUR NEIGHBORS IN JAPAN

OUR NEIGHBORS IN KOREA

Communism in Our World

JOHN C. CALDWELL

With a foreword by

HARRY D. GIDEONSE

President, Brooklyn College

Revised Edition

The John Day Company

New York

Foreword

MORE than 1,000,000,000 people live in countries that are in communist control. Since the United States is the only country powerful enough to stand in the way of the persistent and determined effort of the communists to control the world, we have become the special target of communist propaganda everywhere. A whole generation of our youth is called to contribute a valuable slice of its best years to military service here and throughout the world. A very large part of our taxes—in the past, in the present, and into the future as far as we can now foresee—is spent to meet the cost of our defense preparations, and to give assistance and military strength to our partners in the defense of free nations throughout the world.

Clearly, communism is one of the major facts of life to young Americans. If we are to defend our own conception of a free society effectively we must learn to understand our ideals and our present achievements in the light of an informed comparison with communist theories and communist practice. John C. Caldwell, the author of *Communism in Our World,* speaks from an extensive experience with communism throughout the world, and especially in the Far East and Korea. His simple description of communist theory and communist practice throughout the world will help us to clarify our understanding—and our faith—in the free and democratic way of life.

HARRY D. GIDEONSE

Contents

Introduction

ON July 29, 1955, three tearful young men stepped off a ship in San Francisco. William Cowart, age twenty-two; Otho Bell, age twenty-four, and Lewis Griggs, age twenty-three, were truly men without country. Two years earlier they had renounced America to become "workers for peace" in Communist China; now they had changed their minds and come back to America.

The bewildered young Americans had little to say. They had to their credit the fact that they at last saw the light, were willing to face the music and come home to the land they had betrayed. Otho Bell did make a short statement. Just before being led off by military police he said, *"If I had really been educated before I left this country and known what communism really was, I would have been killed on the Korean battlefields rather than become a prisoner of war."*

Otho Bell was one of the twenty-one young Americans who chose communism at the Panmunjom repatriation center in 1953.

But in addition to the twenty-one who stayed, there were nearly a thousand more young American soldiers, both officers and enlisted men, whose actions while in communist military prisons were suspect. Some of them have already been acquitted of wrong-doing, others have been court-martialed, still others are under investigation.

I have written this book not in condemnation of Otho Bell and the other twenty who stayed behind, but in the hope that it will help prevent more such tragedies in the future. The case histories of these young Americans, brilliantly written by Virginia Pasley in her book *Twenty-One Stayed,* reveal many reasons why American soldiers broke when faced with months of brainwashing. Over and over again, as Mrs. Pasley interviewed parents, teachers, and pastors, she heard this refrain: "If only he had known about politics, if only he had known about communism."

The report of the Secretary of Defense's Advisory Committee on Prisoners of War, released August 17, 1955, has some pertinent things to say about the lack of information and education of young Americans faced with communism. Parts of this report follow:

> When plunged into a communist indoctrination mill, the average American POW was under a serious handicap. Enemy political officers forced him to read Marxian literature. He was compelled to participate in debates. He had to tell what he knew about American politics and American history. And many times the Chinese and Korean instructors knew more about these subjects than he did . . . A large number of American POW's did not know what the communist program was all about . . . A great many servicemen were teen-agers. At home they had thought of politics as dry editorials or uninteresting speeches, dull as ditchwater. Some of the POW's had heard of communism only as a name. Many had never before heard of Karl Marx . . . The Committee heard evidence which revealed that many POW's knew too little about the United States and its ideals and traditions . . .
> The Committee heard numbers of ex-POW's who stated that a knowledge of communism would have enabled them to expose its fallacies . . . These men had lost their battle before they entered the service . . . In a war for the minds of men, the enemy's methods can be successfully combatted by military training and civilian education . . . In battle and in captivity the fighting American is no better than his training and education.
> . . . military skill must be reinforced by will, by moral character and by basic beliefs instilled at home and in the classroom long before the lad enters military service . . .

A book about communism for young people is bound to be controversial. But that does not mean the subject can be avoided. The experience of young Americans in Korea points to the need for them to be better prepared for the world of today. Regardless of "summit" conferences and periods of peaceful coexistence, the menace of communism will be with us for years to come. Surely the most potent and little understood political force in centuries is not too ticklish for young people to read about!

I have not attempted to go deeply into communist theory with its devious twists and turns. Some of the sudden changes in communist line cannot be understood for months, and are subject to widely, differing interpretations by experts in the field. Rather, I have tried to answer in simple language the questions: What is communism? How did it begin? What is it like in actual operation? Why is it bad? What are we doing to protect ourselves?

If these questions can be adequately answered in the minds of American youth, there need be no more Otho Bells with their sad lament, "If I had only known what communism really was." And there need be no more Americans who have lost their battle even before it begins.

Communism in Our World

CHAPTER I

The Cold-War World

OUR country has been at peace for over fifteen years. At least, World War II ended in 1945 and the United States has not been officially at war since that time. But have we, or the rest of the world, really been at peace? Do we live today in a peaceful world?

Today American soldiers, sailors, and airmen are still stationed all over the world. To be exact, 1,016,000 American servicemen were stationed in forty-nine different countries in early 1962. The United States maintains eighty-nine air bases in Europe, Asia, Africa, even in the Arctic. In thirty-four countries groups of American soldiers are stationed to train the fighting forces of those nations, to supervise the use of guns, planes, and ships which our country is giving to other nations so that they can defend themselves.

Certainly this does not sound like a world at

peace, does it? And a nation at peace, in a peaceful world, should not have to spend a very large proportion of its budget on national defense, should it?

America demobilized quickly after the end of World War II. By 1950 our defense budget was down to about twelve billion dollars. Even that is a lot of money. But in 1953 and 1954 our nation spent more than forty billion dollars on guns and ammunition, planes and ships, soldiers, airmen, and sailors, and on developing new and terrible bombs. Our experts tell us that we shall probably spend thirty-five to forty-five billion dollars a year for many years to come—on defense and on machines of war.

During these years of supposed peace, nearly 150,000 American soldiers were killed or wounded in a far-off land called Korea. American pilots have been shot down off the coast of China, over the seas of Japan and the Bering Sea, in the skies over Europe.

Years after the coming of "peace," our country is still drafting young men for military service. It is expected that the draft will continue for several, perhaps many, years to come.

We call this period that is not war and yet not peace, a *cold war*. To understand why we have a cold war it is necessary first to look at the map on pages 20-21 and to understand what has happened to the face of our world.

You will notice that some of the nations of the world are lightly shaded; others are white; still others appear as dark-shaded areas of the map.

The countries in dark shading are under the rule of communism. It is quite apparent that a large portion of the world is now communistic. All or parts of fifteen nations lie within the empire of communism. Nearly one third of the earth's surface lies in communist hands. More than a billion people, or 34 per cent of the world's population, live in these countries.

The map, and the history of one quarter of the earth's surface, provide the reason why the United States is not really at peace. Twelve years ago there was only one communist nation, Russia. But as the years have passed, communism has moved swiftly. Other nations have been gobbled up, more millions of people have been enslaved. Communism has swept some nations by conquest, others by subversion and revolution.

The light-gray areas on the map are the noncommunist nations, many of which have actively banded together to fight against communism.

THE COMMUNIST WORLD

 over 1,000,000,000 people

 living in 16 countries

 covering nearly $\frac{1}{3}$ of the earth's surfa

There are, however, a number of countries which do not have communist governments and which are in many ways unsympathetic to communism but which try to be completely neutral. These nations appear on the map as white areas. The whole world today is lined up in three different camps. Without mentioning many of the lesser nations, the world line-up looks something like this:

Communist Nations	*Anti-Communist Nations*	*Neutrals*
Russia	United States of America	India
Communist China		Indonesia
East Germany	Great Britain	Burma
Poland	Canada	Ceylon
Bulgaria	Australia	Egypt
Rumania	France	Numerous
Czechoslovakia	Italy	other newly
North Korea	Spain	independent
North Vietnam	Japan	nations of
Hungary	Greece	Africa
Yugoslavia	Turkey	
Cuba	West Germany	
	Nationalist China	
	South Korea	

It is the tension caused by this division of nations that leads the United States to spend so much for arms, to keep one million men overseas, to maintain eighty-nine great air bases on foreign soil. It is not only a struggle to stay strong. There is a continuous struggle to keep smaller nations from losing to the communists. Both the free world and the communist world are also engaged in a contest to sway the thinking of people living in the neutral countries.

As nations and people have fallen to communism, millions of innocent men and women have lost their lives. Hundreds of thousands of people have been tortured and executed without trial. More millions have been made hungry or desperately unhappy.

We might argue that the misery, even the death, of people living in faraway countries, should make Americans uneasy for their own safety. But even more important in the long run than the misery of millions is this fact: The leaders of world communism have time and again stated that they will not be satisfied until they control all the world.

The United States is the only nation powerful enough to stand in the way of a communist-dominated world. It has, therefore, become the special target of the communists. This fact has forced America to stay strong, to spend billions for defense in a time of supposed peace. Since even America needs allies, we must also keep our fighting men in other countries, to strengthen and to train. Since the communist nations might strike us at any moment, we must maintain air bases all over the world, with planes capable of striking back quickly. At home we must be constantly on guard also. For the communists have conquered many people by what we call subversion as well as by outright attack.

The purpose of this book is to find out what communism is, why it is dangerous to all peace-loving people, and why it is especially a threat to America.

We shall find out not only what communism is but how it operates. How and when did it begin? Why, in a little over fifteen years, has it spread to nearly a third of the world's surface? What is our government doing to stop its march? What can we, as American citizens, do?

As we learn about communism we shall learn, too, the meaning of new words and phrases that it has brought into use. A few years ago there was no such phrase as *cold war*. The communists have given new meaning to the word *subversion*. They have invented something called *brainwashing*. They have set us talking about *coexistence*.

Communism has changed the lives of millions of people. In many ways it has already changed the lives of Americans. Political experts tell us that it may be a world force for another generation, perhaps for another century. It is time, then, that we learn as much as possible about it.

During 1960 and 1961, communism became a greater threat to the United States than ever before. In 1960, our President met with Nikita Khrushchev, and for a while there was hope of better relations. Unfortunately, soon after the meeting an American plane called the U-2 was shot down over Russia. If our country is to remain secure, we must know what the Russians are doing. It is necessary to gather intelligence about the enemy, and this is what the U-2 was doing. The Russians used the U-2 incident as an excuse to change completely their attitude toward our country.

Russia began to do its utmost to cause trouble throughout Africa and particularly in the former Belgian colony, now an independent nation called the Congo Republic. Both Russia and Communist China began to give help to the new government that came to power in Cuba. This country only ninety miles off our coast is now under communist control.

The communists have succeeded in threatening several countries in Southeast Asia. During 1961 and 1962, relations between our country and Russia were further threatened because of Russia's efforts to force our country and our allies out of West Berlin.

CHAPTER II

What Is Communism?

THE dictionary defines communism as "any theory of social organization which advocates common ownership of all agents of production, and some approach to an equal distribution of the products of industry."

Putting this definition into everyday words, communism is a system under which everybody has an equal share in factories, farms, and stores. Everyone shares equally in the crops produced on farms. Everyone shares equally in the things made by factories. Since everyone shares alike, there is no need for private ownership. All things are jointly owned by all citizens.

In such a system there would be no poor people, no rich people. The hard worker would receive the same share as the lazy man. No one would ever starve, everyone would have sufficient clothing and proper housing.

Perhaps this does not sound like too bad a way of life. There would be no poverty, no need for some people to receive relief checks from the government. No one could become very rich but on the other hand no one would be poor. No man could own a vast factory employing thousands of other men and women. If one man were fortunate enough to invent something of great value, all others would share in the good things brought by the invention.

For centuries this idea of society has appealed to people.

The Bible tells us that the early Christians attempted at one time to form a communist society. The fourth chapter of Acts describes how "those who believed were of one heart and soul, and no one said that any of the things which he possessed was his own, but they had everything in common." The experiment worked for a while, the Bible says: "There was not a needy person among them, for as many as were possessors of lands or houses sold them, and brought the proceeds of what was sold and laid it at the apostles' feet; and distribution was made to each as he had need."

But even among devout Christians the experiment in communism was not successful. First of all, a man named Ananias and his wife Sapphira sold a piece of property,but kept back a part of the proceeds. Perhaps this couple had a large amount of property and were unwilling to share everything with the others. They were especially condemned because they lied, saying they had contributed all they owned when they had not. At any rate, we know that the early Christians soon gave up the idea of communistic living.

Since Biblical times we have many other records of people who have tried to establish communistic societies. Several such experiments have been tried at various times in America. All have failed eventually. There are too many people like Ananias and his wife, unwilling to share everything they own with others. There are too many lazy people who will not do their share of work if they know that they will be fed and clothed without working. There are always people of great ability and ambition. They dislike to share alike with others who do no work.

We might think that since small experiments in communism have failed, it would be useless for whole nations to try it. As a matter of fact, as we read further, we will find that the nations which say they are communist are failing to set up a communal society. As it has turned out, people in those countries do not share alike, are not in any way equal.

Instead of being systems of government under which there is equality and sharing in all things, the communist countries have become lands of oppression. But that is a part of the story of communism that we will look into later.

Communism in the form we know today is a little over one hundred years old. We might add that there is still no real communist government. Even the Russian communists say that they have only reached a stage in the road to communism which they call *socialism*. However, since the word *communism* is so widely used in the world today we too shall use it to describe the form of government in Russia and the other nations allied with Russia. And communism as we thus think of it today had its beginnings in 1848 when Karl Marx and Friedrich Engels published a little book called *The Communist Manifesto*.

Karl Marx is the better known of the two men. The communist idea of government and society is often called Marxism because of him. Marx was born in Germany in 1818 and died in 1883.

He was in trouble most of his life. In 1849 the German government tried him for treason. He was acquitted but was expelled from Germany. Marx settled in London and lived there the rest of his life.

In addition to writing *The Communist Manifesto,* Marx edited communist magazines. He was a leader in the International Working Men's Society. He taught that the workingman must turn upon his employer. Once the workingmen of the world were in control, they would set up a new social order where all men would be equal. All classes of people would merge into one class.

Karl Marx called this new order "the dictatorship of the proletariat." The communists often use this phrase. It means a government dictated and run by the common people. But at the same time the communists stress that the government must be led by the very few who are actually party members.

Marxism appealed to many people—in Europe, even in America. We must remember that the world of a century ago was quite different from the world we know. When Karl Marx wrote his manifesto, the condition of workingmen everywhere was bad. New machines were being invented, new things manufactured. Thousands of people in Europe left their farms to work in the new factories.

There were no laws then to protect the rights of working people. Children worked twelve and fifteen hours a day. Factory conditions were poor; wages were low. There was insufficient housing for the new workers, and people lived in miserable slums. People were being exploited and it is natural that the teachings of Marx were eagerly accepted by many men and women.

In the fifty years after the publication of Karl Marx's writings, his ideas were discussed all through the world. Marxist, or, as they were more often called, socialist, political parties, were organized in most of the countries of Europe and in America. However, as working conditions improved, most socialists decided that revolutions were not needed; reforms could be achieved by men and women working together in political organizations. Karl Marx, however, wrote of obtaining better conditions by revolution — by fighting.

Even after his death in 1883, Karl Marx continued to have great influence. He became the apostle of the socialist and Marxist parties all over the world. Different men interpreted his writings in different ways.

There were Marxists in many countries. Sometimes they caused trouble, but for the most part people preferred to work peacefully for reforms. However, in one country the seeds of communism as we know it today were being planted. That country was Russia.

Russia was the most backward of all the great European nations. The people of Russia had been ruled by the czars for many years. The czars were rich, powerful, and cruel. They ruled by means of a huge army and police force. The workers and the farmers of Russia had few rights, were barely able to make a living. The reforms that had come to America and most European countries came much more slowly in Russia.

It was natural, then, that the ideas of Marx should interest Russians. Here and there Russians began to band together in secret political groups. They studied the writings of Karl Marx, began to publish secret newspapers. These activities were dangerous, because the czarist police were everywhere. Anyone who was caught working against the czars was immediately imprisoned or exiled to Siberia.

The two chief leaders of these early communists were Nicolai Lenin* and Leon Trotsky. These men did not call themselves communists, however. Their party was named the Social Democratic Labor Party. Operating in secret, driven and persecuted by the police, they did not have much success until World War I.

During that war, Russia suffered many casualties. Near the end of the war conditions became unbearable. Hundreds of thousands of people were starving to death; sickness swept the land. The Russians who had suffered so long under the czars rebelled. The army was sick of fighting and refused to obey the Czar's orders.

On March 15, 1917, the Czar was forced to abdicate his throne, and Russia became a free and democratic nation. In a way, we might compare the revolution in Russia with our own revolution against England. We, too, were oppressed and had little voice in our government. Our revolution was also carried on by patriotic men and women who wanted a better way of life.

The overthrow of the czars was not brought about by the communists, even though they

*Although generally known, even among communists, as Nicolai Lenin, his real name was Vladimir Ilitch Lenin.

claim that to be the case. There were thousands of patriotic Russians who made the revolution possible. They wanted a democratic government like the United States. As soon as the Czar was overthrown, plans were made for free elections and a democratic form of government. The United States was the first nation in the world to recognize and encourage the new Russian government.

Unfortunately, two things made it difficult for the people of Russia to have a real democracy. First, most of the people were uneducated, and they had been oppressed for so long that they went wild. Thousands of farmers who had worked for rich landowners killed their masters. Workmen stormed the factories and took over. Everywhere in Russia there was killing, murder, looting. There was no discipline and no planning, no one to take over and see that order was maintained. That is, there was no one, or no political party, with plans as well organized as the followers of Karl Marx.

There were only a few thousand of these in Russia, but, as has happened in many other countries since, they were able to take control. With Lenin and Trotsky as leaders, the communists, as they soon began to call themselves, had control of Russia within a few months. They had planned and schemed for years; they knew how to take advantage of the terrible conditions in Russia. The democratic government which had been established when the Czar abdicated was overthrown. Communism cannot exist in a truly free nation, so the new rulers of Russia quickly abolished freedom of the press. The leaders of all other political parties were arrested.

The majority of the educated Russian people were not in favor of the methods used by Lenin and Trotsky. Most of them wanted a true democracy; yet for nearly four years the people suffered under terror worse than anything they had experienced under the czars.

It is impossible to know how many people were murdered and executed. The communists ruthlessly wiped out people who opposed them. Both the army and the navy rebelled against the communists. But the communist organization was excellent. With the help of its secret police called the *Cheka,* and with its own army, it was able to defeat all its enemies.

When the Russian Revolution began in 1917, there were few actual communists. These few were able to win out over millions of people who were opposed to them. They won, not only because they were well organized and knew how to take advantage of every situation, but also because they used *terror* as a weapon. We shall see as we go along that communism has won other countries in the same manner. A few men, well organized, with well-laid plans, using terror and murder, have been able to take over country after country. They have succeeded because their opposition has been divided and without organization. But always terror and the secret police are an important part of communist strategy. Lenin was not ashamed of his methods. He told his comrades, "Terror cannot be dispensed with."

In early 1921, Lenin's program had succeeded and the communists were in complete control of Russia. This does not mean that they had the support of the people. They ruled, but many Russians hated their new rulers just as much as they hated the czars. Not only did the communists have trouble with their people, they had trouble among themselves.

As in the Bible story of Ananias and Sapphira, there were communists who did not do their share, who were in it for personal gain. There were honest differences of opinion among the leaders: some communists believed that the party should first succeed completely in Russia before trying to make all the world communist, while others advocated the cause of immediate world revolution. There were many rivalries, too, among the top communists. Usually the man who controlled the secret police was in a position to control his rivals.

Trouble among the communist leaders began as soon as they had achieved control over all Russia. Leon Trotsky, one of the original leaders and the first leader of the Red Army, lost out and fled. Many of the leading communists were imprisoned or executed when their rivals got the upper hand.

Josef Stalin was one of the most ambitious and clever of the early communists. Even though he and Lenin did not get along, Stalin was able to take over control of the Communist Party. Using the secret police, he kept his power by arresting other communist bosses, or sometimes by having them murdered. By 1940, more than half of the original members of the communist executive committee had been executed. Often, forced by torture, these men admitted crimes they had never committed. Hundreds of communists were convicted of treason.

Since many people were executed without trial, it is impossible to know how many communists have been killed by other communists. It is known that during one period more than thirty thousand officers of the Red Army were executed. Thousands of people, officers, party members, sometimes high officials, were sent off to imprisonment in slave labor camps.

The struggle between the top communists has continued to the present time. It has become a part of the life of all other communist countries. The latest case of a top Russian communist's being "purged" took place in 1953. Lavrenti Beria, for many years a high officer in the secret police and finally one of the top three communists after Stalin died, was arrested in 1953. Six months after his arrest it was announced that he had been executed, after confessing to many crimes.

In 1956 Russian leaders began a program to discredit Josef Stalin. We might say that Stalin too has been purged. His body has even been removed from its place of honor in Moscow and placed in a new grave.

The purging and execution of communist leaders show how it is necessary to use terror to keep a communist government in power. Imagine a situation in which the President of the United States would suddenly have the Vice-President arrested! Or in which the Speaker of the House of Representatives would be put on trial and confess to treason or to being a secret agent for another country!

Yet this is a part of government life in every communist-ruled nation. It is important to understand, because the communists call their governments democratic, too. Some of the communist nations use names such as "People's Democratic Republic" or "People's Republic."

A government which must use terror and frequent purging of its leaders does not sound democratic, does it? Yet people all over the world have been deceived by communism. Even in America there have been men and women who believed that the communists were really democratic leaders, giving their nations governments that made life better for the citizens.

After all, the communist ideal of equality for all, of government by the people themselves, sounds attractive. And what could be more democratic? But it is important now to see how communism actually operates. Do the people really control their governments? Has communism made life better for its more than nine hundred million people? Is there any true democracy in communist nations?

There are people living in the free nations who believe that the brutal days of communism are over. They believe that the communists have kept their promises. They believe that the communists are not a threat to the rest of the world.

So we shall visit typical communist countries to see what life under communism is like, to learn how communist-style "democracy" works.

CHAPTER III

Communism in Practice

BEFORE we study the day-to-day operation of a communist government we should make a distinction between the rulers and the ordinary citizens of a communist nation. Our criticisms of communism should not be directed at the common people. Many, perhaps most, of the people in communist nations desire a different type of government. Certainly most of them have been caught in the communist net and we do not criticize them for a way of life they do not want.

With this distinction in mind, let us take a look at the communist government of Russia. Officially Russia is called the Union of Soviet Socialist Republics, shortened to USSR. The word *soviet* was originally used to describe the council or governing body of a communist organization. Now it is often used in the same way we use the word *communist*. We speak of "the Soviet Army," "the Soviets," or "the Soviet government."

The official name suggests that the Russian system is something like our United States. There are a number of republics in the Russian union, just as there are forty-eight states in the American union.

There is a national constitution which, as does the American constitution, provides that the member states have certain rights. The Russian constitution also guarantees many individual rights. According to the constitution, the people have the rights of free speech, assembly, and religion just as Americans have these rights. Elections are held regularly in Russia and other communist nations.

There are many similarities between the constitution of Russia and those of truly democratic nations. The rights of all people, regardless of race, color, and religion, are guaranteed. The right of people to select their officials in free elections is included.

But these similarities are only in the wording of the constitution. The truth is that the citizens of Russia have few of the rights which we take for granted. From birth until death the average citizen lives under the authority of his government. In many cases the government decides how one is to be educated. The government decides what job the average worker shall take. By restricting travel it is possible also to decide where a person shall live. And all the supposed rights of the communist citizen can be taken away at a moment's notice. For there is a big "if" in the communist-style constitution.

The "if" of the constitution is the statement that the citizen's rights can be exercised only in the interests of the working people and "in order to strengthen the socialist system."

To understand what this means, think what life in the United States would be like if our constitution gave every citizen the right to live as he wished, to work, worship, speak, and read freely, "as long as nothing he does interferes with the welfare of the Democratic or Republican Party."

And it is the communist government that has the right to decide whether a person's activities are in the interests of the "working class." Remember that it is a part of communist theory that a few people at the top shall make the important decisions.

And the people at the top have a powerful weapon to enforce their decisions. The communist system provides that any person who is considered socially dangerous can be exiled without trial. The Soviet Criminal Codex, or law, further states that a person can be exiled (which means being sentenced to a slave-labor camp) even if he has been tried for a crime and has been acquitted.

Mr. Robert Kennedy, who became the attorney general of the United States in 1961, made a long trip to Russia in 1955 and told of his findings in the magazine *U. S. News and World Report* (October 21, 1955). Mr. Kennedy made a special study of Soviet law. He reported that there is a board within the Ministry of Interior (which runs the secret police) that has the power to sentence a man to five years in a labor camp. After the sentence has been served, the board can extend it for another five years, without a trial.

Mr. Kennedy also reported that many exceptions to the constitution are made in cases of people arrested for political reasons, or suspected of being "enemies of the state." Special secret courts are set up to try such cases. Hundreds of thousands of Russians have been exiled and imprisoned without open trials.

The Russian government has another powerful weapon that goes along with this right to condemn citizens even if they have not committed a crime: the secret police.

You will remember that the early communists used the secret police to gain control of Russia. The secret police has remained a powerful part of the government. Originally called the Cheka, it has had various names. But the purpose is always the same, to keep track of every Russian citizen so that he will "stay in line."

There are only between six million and seven million Communist Party members among the more than two hundred million people of Russia. Very different is our situation in America, where there are tens of millions of registered Republicans and Democrats. Since people in our country vote freely, control of the government can and does pass from one political party to the other. But in Russia there is only one party, and it does not have enough members to control the people. The secret police thus is an important part of the communist system. It helps accomplish what a small political party itself cannot accomplish.

No one but the highest officials of the Russian

government knows how many men and women are employed in the secret police. It is known that there are secret police in every army unit, factory, and school. It is their job to listen in on conversations, to read people's mail, to find out what books or magazines are being read, and whether Russians are listening to radio broadcasts from foreign countries.

The secret police have even been helped by children. Since communism teaches that one's first obligation is to the communist government and not to his family, there have been frequent cases of children denouncing their parents to the police.

The long arm of the communist secret police reaches into every hour of every person's life. The Soviet government naturally tries to keep secret the number of its citizens who have been exiled to slave-labor camps, and it surrounds the camps with secrecy so that the outside world cannot know about conditions there. But prisoners escape and a few have been voluntarily released. From their stories we know that at least twenty-five million people have been sentenced to slave labor. We cannot know how many are actually now in the camps, but reliable estimates run all the way from five million to twenty-five million.

Working often in the bitter cold of Siberia, sometimes within the Arctic Circle, thousands of men and women have died for lack of food and medical attention, or because of brutal treatment. The slave laborers have been used to build great new air bases, to dig canals, to mine uranium. Remember that most of them are not guilty of criminal offenses. They have only been guilty of failure to agree with the communist government. Perhaps the offense has been nothing more than a conversation overheard and reported to the police.

There has been great material progress in Russia. But it is well to remember that much of it has been made possible by slave labor. Writing about the material progress in parts of Russia, Mr. Robert Kennedy says: "But I think also the price that was paid in human beings in order to make this change and, too, that the people have such a difficult life even now, should be considered.

"Sections of the population were banished or liquidated [executed] to achieve the domination of the state. The breaking down of family life is effectively carried out by mothers working for the state and depositing their babies . . . in state nurseries, later in Pioneer camps and, ultimately, in the Young Communists League. During this most important formative period the children and the young people are being thoroughly indoctrinated that their first love should be the state, not God, their parents or their family."

The secret police have developed methods of operation unknown in other civilized countries. The communists believe that a terror-stricken people can be easily managed. Through terror, the will to resist and to fight back can be controlled. So from time to time the police make arrests, or haul people off for questioning. Generally they act late at night. "The knock on the door at night" has come to millions of people in all communist-ruled nations. At two or three o'clock in the morning, there is a sudden knock. The husband or wife is barely given time to get dressed. There is no warrant for arrest, no explanations are given. Sometimes the person is questioned briefly, then sent home, or there may be hours of questioning and torture. But sometimes the person simply disappears. His family never hears from him again.

The secret police have developed many torture methods. Among them is the mental torture we call *brainwashing,* which we shall read about in detail in another section.

It is clear that the rights granted by a communist-style constitution do not mean much. It can be understood, too, why nearly 100 per cent of the people in Russia vote for the Communist Party. Not only are they afraid not to, there is only one candidate for each office. The candidate, whether for a national office or for a local office, is selected by the Party. Even if voters dared to do so, there is no opportunity to exercise choice when there is only one candidate.

In some communist nations voting is even less "free." In communist North Korea there was an election in 1948. Each voting place contained a white ballot box and a black ballot box. A communist policeman stood between the two ballot boxes. The voter could vote for the Party's candidate, in which case he placed his ballot in the white box. If he wished to vote against him, he could place his ballot in the black box. The policeman, of course, knew which way each person voted. But even with this control, some voters had the courage to vote against the candidate. As soon as they left the voting place they were followed to their homes and arrested.

In one town where numerous people voted no, the result was still announced as 100 per cent for the Party. In fact the communists sometimes go too far in announcing the total vote. In one district in Russia it was announced that Josef Stalin had received 111 per cent of the total votes. In other words, he got more votes than there were voters!

Yes, we can agree that Russia and the other communist nations have democratic constitutions. These read somewhat like the Constitution of the United States. But there are great differences in practice. In a true democracy, government exists for the good of the people. In a communist-style democracy the people exist for the government.

Even so, we may argue that life is better in Russia or Communist China or Communist Poland now than it was before communism. People who are friendly to the communists often argue this way. They say that in spite of harsh rule, people are happier because they have better lives now than they once did. So let us see how typical workers and farmers live in Russia and the other communist nations. There are many refugees from these nations who have told their stories. So we are not guessing. We know how people live in the communist world.

CHAPTER IV

"The Workers' Paradise"

WE HAVE already learned that the vote of a Russian citizen means nothing because there is no choice. This lack of choice is one of the most important differences between communist-style democracy and real democracy. Earlier we mentioned that in communist practice it is the few top party members that must control the government, since the common people are unable to understand communism.

The few men at the top have a great deal of control over the daily lives of all citizens. Normally a Russian worker cannot quit a job of his own accord. The penalty can be a sentence of ten years at slave labor. A Russian boy may be drafted for labor at the age of fourteen. Each year between 800,000 and 1,000,000 boys *and girls* are drafted into jobs. For four years after completing vocational training, the young Russian must take the job selected for him.

If a young Russian worker is absent for as much as twenty minutes, he may be transferred to a lower-paying job. He cannot strike. To do so might bring a death sentence.

In judging conditions of life under the communists, we must realize that changes have taken place. First, the Russian government has eased some of the many restrictions placed upon its citizens. Russians now have more opportunity to buy goods for their homes. There is somewhat more freedom of expression. But most experts on communism believe that the government still exercises a great deal of control over the lives of all the people.

Secondly, we must understand that different people have quite different opinions about Russia and communism. The information we get from Russia comes from various sources: newspaper reporters who have been assigned there; university professors in America who teach courses on communism; travelers to Russia; persons who have escaped from Russia and are now living in the free world.

Mr. Harrison Salisbury, who lived in Russia for several years as a correspondent for the *New York Times,* states that except for students who are given special technical training, workers in

Russia now have a free choice of jobs. However Mr. Robert Kennedy, who traveled extensively in Russia in 1955, says they do not have a free choice. Mr. Salisbury believes that there is now increasing freedom for Russians to travel in their own country. Mr. Kennedy says there is very little such freedom. And Mr. Nikolai Khokhlov, a former Soviet intelligence officer who escaped to the United States in 1954, reported in *U. S. News and World Report* (March 30, 1956): "Everybody in the Soviet Union has to have a passport to move from one house to another. The farmer doesn't have any passport or any documents at all. He cannot leave his village, except for an occasional temporary leave of one or two days —to sell his potatoes at market, for instance— and then he has to go back. Tens of millions are actually imprisoned on their farms."

Finally, in addition to difference of opinion, there is another difficulty in getting exact information on conditions. This is that while the law may state that a citizen has a certain right, in practice it is always possible to "forget about the law." The Communist Party supersedes the law.

Even though conditions have improved, the lot of the average Russian is still hard. Normally, he must take the job the government wants him to take. Hours are long, discipline is severe, punishment is harsh. There is little the Soviet citizen can buy with his money. While there is no rationing as such in Russia, there are few things to buy. And prices are very high.

Visitors to Russia report that it is a common sight to see long lines of people in front of stores, waiting for a chance to buy things. So although there is no actual rationing, the effect is the same. Nikolai Khokhlov describes how a man goes about buying a suit in Russia *(U. S. News and World Report,* March 30, 1956): "He has to hunt for days and days and is lucky if he finds a store where maybe tomorrow morning there will be some good suits for sale. And he has to take a day off and perhaps stay all night in this store to get on a list—they sometimes put down the names of hundreds of people on a piece of paper, and they wait all night. There are, maybe, a hundred suits—and they are snapped up quickly. And some who waited all night will not get any."

The Communist government controls housing and food distribution and can favor people that cooperate with the government. In America any citizen can go to a store and buy whatever food he can afford. But in communist countries people eat what their governments tell them to eat. And always the government has the power to starve people.

The worker in America can buy what he pleases. He can live where he wishes. He can rent a house or an apartment or he can buy a home. Twenty-four million American families live in homes they own.

In Russia the government owns the apartment houses and many homes. A Russian worker with a wife and two children generally is allowed a space eighteen feet square for housing his family. The bathroom and kitchen must be shared with other families. This means that the family has 324 square feet of living space.

To understand the crowded way in which the average Russian family lives, compare this living area with that of a typical small American house. If it has two bedrooms, living-dining room, kitchen, and bath, the total area of the house will be between 750 and 1,200 square feet. This means that an American workingman, wife and two children have about 250 square feet of living space for each person. The Russian worker has one third as much.

The typical American family has a radio, and

very frequently a TV set. There are nearly 50,000,-000 telephones in the United States. Almost every family has an automobile. Here is an interesting figure: In 1959, 5,599,000 cars were produced in the United States. It is estimated that about 500,-000 are produced annually in Russia.

Americans are exceptionally well off, but people can be happy without all the luxuries Americans enjoy. We mention how little the average Russian has by comparison because the communists frequently boast that they have given their people a better life than that of workers in America. They describe American workers as down-trodden people, so poorly paid they cannot even buy sufficient food for their families. But the truth is that under the democratic system Americans receive better pay, are better housed and fed, and work shorter hours than the people of Russia. Even more important than these material things is the fact that Americans need not fear secret police. With all the good things of life we also enjoy freedom that is unknown in any communist country.

We must not suppose that Russia is a poor country without natural resources. Actually Russia is rich in natural resources, including minerals, oil, lumber, and fertile soil. The Russian government has built new hydroelectric plants, irrigation systems, factories. But the factories produce heavy machinery, guns, tanks, and airplanes. Cars and trucks are made for the use of the army or for government officials and not for ordinary citizens.

Remember that the goal of communism is a "workers' paradise," a classless society where everyone shares equally in the good things of life. Yet there is a greater difference between classes in communist countries than in most other countries. While the average person is barely able to make a living, members of the Communist Party, high government officials, the secret police, and some skilled engineers lead an entirely different life. They enjoy luxuries unknown to the common people, having private cars and luxurious apartments

Some officials in Russia receive incomes of a million rubles a year. Among workers there is a great difference in salaries paid. In 1955 two Americans, Dr. Homer Dodge and Mr. Norton Dodge, made a study of incomes in Russia. Here are some of the results. (Although one ruble is supposed to be worth twenty-five cents, because things cost so much the ruble has a real value of less than ten cents.)

An unskilled workman receives 138 rubles a week (equivalent to about $11.00), or just under 7,200 rubles a year; experienced high-school teacher, 15,600 rubles a year; experienced engineer, 30,000 rubles a year; manager of a big store, 42,000 rubles a year; manager of a large manufacturing plant, 145,000 rubles a year.

In other words, there is no classless society, no real sharing. The rulers live in luxury; the average citizen is poor. Members of the Communist Party receive higher salaries and more privileges than the millions who are not party members. This is the situation wherever the communists govern a country.

Communism boasts that in addition to offering a better life to industrial workers it also offers much to the farmer. In Russia and China, the two most powerful communist nations, farmers have always had a difficult life. Remember that under the czars few Russians owned their land. Much of the land was held by large landowners. Most farmers had to rent their tiny plots and pay very high rates for them. One of the most popular communist slogans has been "Land for

"EQUALITY" IN RUSSIA
(Comparative yearly salaries)

Party bosses
up to 1,000,000 rubles a year

Factory managers 145,000 rubles a year

Engineers 30,000 rubles a year

Experienced teachers 15,600 rubles a year

Unskilled workers 7,200 rubles a year

the tiller," meaning that those who work the land should own it.

But has communism benefited the average farmer? In Russia millions of farmers have been forced into *collective farms*. A collective farm is a large operation, with all land, buildings and equipment belonging to the government. Each farmer is allowed a very small plot for himself. The law provides he may keep this land forever; but there is a catch, for the law adds that he must farm the land in the way in which the government tells him to farm it. In 1956 the government relaxed regulations to some degree, giving the farmer more control over his individual plot.

In addition to working his own small plot, the farmer on a collective farm must spend much time on the collective acres. He has a compulsory delivery quota. This means that the government tells him exactly how many bushels of each crop he must deliver to the government. The government also sets the price which the farmer will receive.

In other words, the Russian farmer, like the Russian worker, is controlled by the state. He is allowed to "own" a small plot of land, but only as long as he obeys orders. The law even provides that he may buy or build a five-room house. But the government has the power to take the house away if it wishes.

Without any right to his farm, the Russian peasant has little initiative. While farming methods have improved in most of the world, Russian farming is still inefficient. For instance, the average American farmer can raise food for eighteen people; the average Russian farmer is able to raise enough food for three people.

Numerous American farming experts have visited Russia, and several groups of Russian farmers have toured American farms. Americans report that farming in Russia is still many years behind farming in our country. Visitors to Russia have been amazed at the inefficiency they have noted. As an example, often in Russia two drivers and two or three assistants are required to operate one tractor.

Mr. John M. Jacobs, an Arizona cattle rancher who also grows vegetables, fruit and grain, said that after traveling 7,500 miles in Russia he did not get a single idea that would improve his farm.

These observations are important because the communists have bragged a great deal about their accomplishments. Communist propaganda tells the world that only under the communist system are people efficient and happy. The communists frequently claim that everything they do is done better than in America.

But the truth is quite the opposite. The Russian farmer has much less than the American farmer. He is not as efficient. Most Russian farm homes have three or four poorly furnished rooms. Of course, such things as electric appliances are almost unknown. The Russian farmer does not own his tractor, nor any of his major equipment. These things are the property of the state.

In most communist countries farmers are inefficient and badly off. Czechoslovakia, which was once self-sufficient in food, now must import food. Prices have risen. Farmers in communist East Germany and in Poland are unable to produce the food needed or to equal the production enjoyed before these countries became communist-controlled.

In Asia, communism also appealed especially to the farmers. But in Communist China and Communist North Korea the life of farmers is worse now that at any time in history. In 1955 two communist pilots deserted from the North Korean air force, escaping by flying their planes to Seoul in South Korea. These two men, Captain Woon Yong Lee and Lieutenant Eun Seung

Lee, described conditions in that Communist country. Captain Lee said: "People are skin and bones or terribly swollen because they eat food not fit for human beings. People swarm around army mess halls and fight for garbage." Lieutenant Lee told of seeing children fighting with pigs for slop.

China has never been able to produce enough food for its people. Now a combination of floods and droughts and communist inefficiency has created serious problems. Millions of Chinese are either starving or have too little food to keep them healthy. The system by which the government has complete control of the farmers and the land has not worked in China or in any other country.

There are other things in life besides food and wages. While there is actual starvation in some communist countries, let us admit that conditions in Russia may be better than when Russia was ruled by the czars. But what of the other things that make life happy and full? If people are to be contented they must be able to enjoy freedom of religion, freedom to think and speak, and opportunity to have a family life, a chance to travel a bit, to take vacations.

First, we will consider religion. Remember that the Russian constitution guarantees freedom of worship. But since the beginning of the communist movement every effort has been made to drive people away from the church. A magazine for Russian teachers states the position in these words: "He [the good teacher] is obliged not only to be an unbeliever himself but also to be an active propagandist of godlessness among others, to be the bearer of ideas of militant proletarian atheism."

The main communist attack against religion has been in the schools. Children are taught to ridicule their parents who go to church. Thousands of ministers and priests have been imprisoned. Many churches have been closed, the buildings often taken over for housing soldiers or to become museums.

The communist fight against religion is directed not only against Christians. Mohammedans have been persecuted. In China, hundreds of Buddhist monasteries have been closed. The priests have been driven out and forced to work in labor gangs.

A citizen of communist countries may still go to church. But it is risky. The churchgoer may be denounced, ridiculed by his children. The government looks upon a religious man or woman with suspicion. Catholic priests who were released from Chinese communist prisons in 1956 report that in Red China there are frequent drives against Christians. In 1955 the Chinese communist government announced the execution of twenty-eight Protestant ministers. In July, 1955, eighteen young Christians of college age were arrested in Peking because they had participated in Holy Communion. They were charged with "resistance to the communist revolution."

Next, the communists have tried to destroy all family life. In Communist China the government decides when a person shall marry. The government must even approve the match.

Once married, a couple may be separated, for often the government will assign married couples to work in different cities. In all communist countries women must do a great deal of work. In Russia women do heavy farm work, run machinery, dig ditches.

With both the father and the mother away from home, children are educated by the government. Even children three or four years old attend government nursery schools. Older children have long school hours. After school is out they must take part in various young-communist organizations. There is little opportunity for family get-togethers, picnics, evenings at the movies together, trips in the country.

The communists have even taken away the freedom to travel and move about. In Communist China, for instance, a person has to have a special permit to spend *one night* away from home.

In America we have complete freedom to travel. Each year, for instance, when the trout season opens or the deer season begins, thousands of fathers take their sons out into the woods. Father and son can camp out, can hunt or fish. The government does not tell them where to go or where not to go. Normally such a week's outing would be impossible for the average Russian. It would probably be considered unpatriotic and wasteful to spend a week in the woods!

Vacation trips are taken by millions of American families. They can go for long cross-country trips by car. They can take ships or planes to foreign lands. During 1956 one and a quarter million American tourists visited foreign countries.

In an average year, only a few thousand Russians leave their country. And most of these are officials. Diplomats must, of course, visit other countries. But for the average citizen of any communist country, travel, just for pleasure, is impossible.

Of course people do get vacations. Communist workers even get completely free vacations. There are workers' rest camps in most communist nations. But normally only those workers who have done outstanding jobs can have *free* vacations. In all communist countries there are "work quotas." If a worker goes over his quota by working many hours overtime, he becomes a hero. He may get extra rations, a free trip to a rest camp. But for the average worker or farmer there is nothing to break the monotony of hard work.

The picture we have painted of life in Russia and the other communist countries is black. Has communism accomplished anything good for people? Has it been all bad?

We can point out accomplishments. The life of the average person in Russia certainly is better than it was thirty years ago. Except for political prisoners who are starved on purpose, people now have enough to eat. Although of poor quality, there is sufficient clothing for everyone. Medical attention is far better than it was before the communists took control. There are more schools in Russia and in other communist countries than ever before. The rate of illiteracy in Russia was once very high. Now nearly every person can read and write.

It is true also that there have been great scientific developments in Russia and that they are ahead of the United States in certain fields. They are training excellent scientists. This is proved by the fact that in 1957 the Russians were able to launch space satellites. It is probable that they have gone ahead of our country in developing certain kinds of missiles. It is true that these developments have come at the expense of the standard of living of average Russians. But they are important and perhaps make Russia more powerful than ever.

We must also realize that the Russians have made great progress in science. They were able to get a man into space long before the United States accomplished the same feat. They have developed powerful rockets. The communists have also improved their countries physically, building miles of railroads and highways, dams, and irrigation systems. Russia and Communist China are more modern and powerful than before communism took over.

But despite claims to the contrary, *the standard of living has been lowered in every country taken over by the communists, except Russia.* And there are experts who claim that Russians are actually no better off than under the czars.

Of what use are railroads and highways if there is no freedom to travel? What advantage is there in being able to read if the government can tell you what to read, can arrest you for reading the wrong books? Of what help are big industrial plants if people do not make enough money to buy the products manufactured?

In studying the communist system and its accomplishments we should remember that a hundred years ago America was backward, too. We had poorly paid workers, long hours, unsanitary conditions. There were rich men who exploited others.

But look at America today. The American, whether he lives on a farm or works in a factory, is the best-fed, best-dressed and best-housed person in the world. This is important to remember: in America we have accomplished everything which the Communists claim to have accomplished (most of which they have not really accomplished) and we still have our freedom too! It has not been necessary to imprison or execute millions of people to give us the highest standard of living in the world.

Let a man who lived in a communist country

describe communism in his own way. Kim Soon Bok, a Korean artist who lived under communist rule in North Korea but who now lives in South Korea, drew the two pictures shown on page 71. The Korean characters on the side of the big ox mean "Government." The other characters mean "The People."

In the top picture Mr. Kim of Korea shows democracy as a system where the *government works for the people.* The lower picture describes communism as Mr. Kim sees it: *a system where all the people work for the government.*

You need only look at the expressions on the people's faces to know which system Mr. Kim prefers.

CHAPTER V

The Communists and World Conquest

IT SHOULD be clear that communism has not done very much for the nations it controls. Though there has been material progress in all communist countries, it has scarcely helped the average man. Although the communists were actually welcomed in some countries because their promises sounded fine, the promises have not been kept and people have become disillusioned. There has never been a free election in any communist country. There cannot be free elections because once people understand what communism is, they do not want it.

We might begin to wonder, then, why America should worry about communism. It has not been able to give people the freedom and plenty that Americans enjoy. One might say, if other people are foolish enough to put up with it, let them. Let the communists go their way while we go ours.

But it is partly because communism has been such a failure that it is dangerous. It is for this very reason that it is difficult for the world to exist half communist and half free. When people living under communism find out what life is like in free countries, they become dissatisfied. Every day people attempt to escape from communist countries. Hundreds of thousands have crossed the borders to freedom. Millions more would do so if they had the opportunity.

What would happen if the communist nations allowed their citizens to travel freely into other countries? Soon the knowledge of communist failure would be widespread in every country. The people, already oppressed, would become more anxious than ever to escape or to overthrow their governments. In fact, the communists are so afraid of desertions that even their top diplomats in other countries are constantly watched and guarded.

The communists must conquer all the world if their way of life is to succeed. To understand this point, let us imagine what it would be like if the United States were a communist nation and Canada a free and democratic nation. In Canada there would be prosperity; the people would be free to live as they liked. They would have freedom of religion, of speech and expression. Right across the border, in America, people would be slaves of a communist government. The farmers would work on collective farms instead of owning their own land. Millions of men and women would be working in slave-labor camps.

If such a situation existed, it would be impossible to keep Americans from escaping to Canada. It would not be possible to keep from Americans the truth of what life was like in Canada. There would be constant dissatisfaction, the chance of revolution. The communist government in America would find it necessary to try to remove the democratic government of Canada.

The communist plan for world conquest is not new. It was announced in 1919 when communist leaders from all over the world met in Moscow. The aim of world communism has not changed since that time. Over and over again its leaders have described that aim in slogans such as "Let us fight for the victory over capitalism of the toilers of the whole world."

The United States, being the richest and most powerful of the free nations, is the greatest enemy of the communists. Before they can realize their goal of a World Soviet Republic, the United

States must be destroyed. Over and over again communist leaders have made this clear in such statements as "The western way of life, typified by the United States, has been doomed by the march of history."

The aim of American communists is the same. They have frankly stated that a World Soviet Republic must be established. They admit that America is to be a part of that republic. Communists in America, as do communists in all other countries, follow that aim and take their orders from Moscow.

We cannot sit back and say: "Let the communists run their part of the world any way they wish. If people want to be communists, that's their business." Russia's leaders continue to threaten our country and other free nations. In 1961 Mr. Khrushchev boasted that in time Russia would bury our country and that it was only a matter of time before Americans too would be living in a communist nation.

To understand the world of today, we need to understand how the communists operate all over the world. We must understand the methods used in trying to conquer other nations.

Beginning many years ago, communist parties

have been established all over the world. In some countries the Communist Party operates openly. In others it is illegal and operates *underground,* or secretly. In France and Italy the Communist Party is not only legal but very powerful. Millions of voters belong to it. In Italy there are two million party members. In France as many as 186 communists have been elected at one time to the National Assembly, consisting of 627 deputies.

In the United States the Communist Party is small, with perhaps twenty-five thousand members. In 1954, Congress passed several communist control laws which in some respects outlaw the party in our country. The communists cannot operate as a political party. They cannot be elected to public office as communists. Many American communists have gone underground to operate in secrecy. However, we must understand that an American can be a communist as long as he does not openly advocate the overthrow of our government by force. While some communists have gone underground to operate, others have not. The Communist newspaper called *The Worker* is still published.

But whether communists operate openly as in France, or in partial secrecy as in the United

States, their aim is the same. Most communists take their orders from Russia. It is the Russian Communist Party which decides what policy shall be followed in each country.

It is this world-wide organization that makes communism difficult for us to understand, for we do not have anything like it. There is no "American Party" at work in communist countries. There are no "freedom parties" taking orders from other nations. But in every nation there is a communist party, taking orders from Moscow. The allegiance of communists is to the party, not to their country. An American communist is first a communist and secondly an American. In this way communists differ from members of other political parties.

For many years after Russia became communist, the party operated openly in most of the world. Party members infiltrated labor unions, newspapers, schools and colleges. Sometimes the party cooperated with existing governments. Sometimes the communists caused strikes and violence. But for the most part, during the period from 1920 to World War II, the communists were laying a foundation for future action. Since most people did not understand communist aims, it was very easy to infiltrate other nations.

In Spain, the communists openly took part in a bloody civil war. And in China the communists were at war with the Nationalist government for many years. But in most countries the communists were content to plan and infiltrate.

It was World War II that brought the beginning of communist expansion all through the world. The United States became an ally of communist Russia in the war against Germany, Italy and Japan. When the war ended, it was necessary for Allied soldiers to occupy the defeated nations. Russia was able to move its soldiers into many countries in Eastern Europe, into Manchuria and North Korea. This was the opportunity the communists had been waiting for.

In countries occupied by the Red Army the communists first offered to establish coalition governments. This means that they suggested that all political parties which had resisted Germany and her allies should take part in the new free governments. The communists were clever. They talked about helping to establish democratic governments. They promised that there would be free elections, free speech.

But always the communists managed to gain control of the police. They had another advantage too. For many years the Communist Party had trained people of every nationality in methods of gaining control of their countries. Special schools are operated in Moscow for this purpose. Immediately after the end of World War II, trained Hungarians, Czechs, Poles, Rumanians moved back to their homelands. With each passing month the control of the police became tighter. The communists were well organized. People opposed to communism were poorly organized and lacked leadership. So, one after another, the nations of Eastern Europe became communist states.

Only in Czechoslovakia did the communists have serious troubles. The Czechs had been among the freest people in Europe and were proud of their freedom. The communists were able to infiltrate the post-war Czech government, but the freedom-loving people began to understand what was happening. They became aroused over a communist plot to assassinate their beloved Foreign Minister, Jan Masaryk. Elections were to be held in 1948, and the communists knew that they could not win the elections.

In early 1948, the communists arranged a popular demonstration against the coalition government. The police, controlled by the communists, quickly put down all opposition. The army was also under communist control. The communists had infiltrated the newspapers. Even though the great majority of the people were anti-communist, the Reds were so well organized that they were able to take over the country. Czechoslovakia then became a communist *satellite*. This means that it became a nation governed by the Czechoslovakian communists but actually controlled by Russia.

We call all the communist nations of Europe, outside Russia, satellites because all are actually governed by Russia. Local communists are named to the important positions in government. But it is Russia, through her army and her vast secret-police network, that actually controls the life of every citizen in every European communist nation.

Russian activities in Europe after the war were in violation of agreements made with the United States. During the war Russia was our ally. We gave the Russians billions of dollars' worth of war materials to help them fight the Germans. The Russians agreed that after the war there should be free elections in Europe so that people could decide what kind of government they wanted.

But the Russians did not live up to these agreements. Furthermore, while we were helping Russia, she was attempting to undermine the United States. During the war many Russians came to the United States to purchase war materials. Using our friendship as a cover-up, Russian agents began to plot against our government.

It was during this time that the Russians managed to establish a spy ring which was able to steal some of our most important atomic secrets. American communists were able to infiltrate our government. Some communists were able to gain important positions from which they could influence American policy.

We mentioned that one of the great communist weapons is the fact that communists everywhere owe allegiance to communism, not to their own country. Every communist, wherever he may be, is working against the legal government of his country.

But in addition to these millions of men and women, the communists have another powerful weapon. The Russian-directed communist spy network is the largest in the world. It is estimated that there are 250,000 communist agents at work. These men and women are helped by another 750,000 people. Many of these are called "fellow travelers." This term means a person who is not a communist party member but who is sympathetic with communism and is used by the communists. There are fellow travelers in every country. One of the best-known clergymen in England is a fellow traveler. He constantly praises the communists. He preaches that communism is good. He is not a communist, but he does not seem to understand all that communism stands for. He is used by the communists.

With 250,000 trained spies, helped by another 750,000 fellow travelers and sympathizers, the communists have a powerful weapon that threatens every free nation.

Communist agents not only gather military information, as in the case of our atomic spies. They have many other methods of causing trouble for free nations. There are some who are trained in sabotage methods. This means that they know how to blow up railways, bridges and factories. Other agents are assigned to infiltrate labor unions, newspapers, and schools. Agents are specially trained to stir up trouble in weak and divided countries. There is even a special school in Moscow which trains agents in methods of murdering, in how to get false confessions from innocent people. Still other agents are trained in blackmail.

It is the responsibility of this great network of agents to prepare the way for communist conquest of the world. The communist network steals military secrets, stirs up strikes and revolutions, attempts to make people lose faith in their governments and their leaders. It operates everywhere, all the time. No country is too small or unimportant for the communists. Money and instructions are sent all over the world.

Along with the network of spies and agents there is a powerful *propaganda* program directed from Moscow. Communist radio broadcasts are beamed all over the world. In nations where the Communist Party is not outlawed, there are communist bookstores, motion-picture theaters and cultural centers. The communists are especially anxious to win converts among young people. Special magazines and books are provided for high school and college students. Communist cells are organized in schools.

Communist propaganda is designed to discredit the democratic way of life. For instance, the United States is described as a country completely ruled by a few rich men. The rest of the world is told that Americans are terribly overworked, do not have enough to eat, are persecuted by the police. During the Korean war the communists claimed that American soldiers murdered thousands of innocent Koreans. It was claimed that American fliers dropped germ bombs on Korean and Chinese cities.

This is a good place to take a look at a communist method called brainwashing. A number of American pilots captured in Korea admitted that they had dropped germ bombs. We know this is not true because the United States has never used such a weapon. How was it, then, that Americans admitted something that was false?

The method used by the communists to make people admit things that are not true is called brainwashing. But brainwashing does even more. It is a method of making people lose faith in their beliefs, their religious convictions, their country.

Sometimes physical torture is used. Frequently prisoners of the communists are beaten and tortured for months until they agree to sign confessions, or to cooperate. But often the torture is not as much physical as mental.

Often the prisoner is placed in a tiny cell alone. He has no room to move about, nothing to read, no one to whom he can talk. A bright electric light is placed in the cell and is never turned off. During the night the prisoner must lie on his back facing the bright light. If he changes his position, a guard forces him into the original position. For days the prisoner receives just enough food to keep him alive. He can never tell when he will be hauled out for questioning. Sometimes, just after the prisoner has fallen asleep, the questioning begins. For hour after hour questions are asked until the prisoner is completely exhausted and has almost lost his reason. There have been cases in which constant questioning was carried on for thirty-six hours.

After days or even months, the prisoner is weak from insufficient food. He has had no real sleep. He has been constantly threatened. Over and over again his captors have accused him of things he did not do. But in his exhausted, starved condition, he begins to believe some of the things he is told. Or just because he cannot possibly stand any more brainwashing, he willingly signs a false confession.

An American missionary in China, brainwashed for many months, finally admitted that he was an American agent working against the communists. He admitted that he had kept a short-wave radio set in his house and had sent secret messages to America with it.

After the missionary was released, it was months before he realized he had signed false confessions. As a result of months of mental torture, he had actually believed that he had been an American agent, that he had owned a secret short-wave radio set.

Brainwashing takes many different forms. The communists first find out all about their prisoner. He is forced to write a long biography. From this they decide on his weaknesses, how best to break his mind and will.

Among the hundreds of American soldiers captured in Korea by the communists, some were thoroughly brainwashed. At the time of the Korean truce, in 1953, twenty-one Americans renounced their country. They chose to stay behind and live with the communists. Two years later three of the twenty-one came back to America. After seeing what communism really was like, they had chosen the American way of life again.

Other Americans came back to this country convinced that communism was a good thing. Still others cooperated with the communists while in prison camps. On the other hand, there were hundreds of American soldiers who refused to cooperate with the communists in any manner. They refused to become traitors even after months of torture and brainwashing.

The Korean war has shown us what kind of enemy we face. Communism with its brainwashing and torture has been able to turn some Americans against their native land. No other enemy our country has ever faced was able to accomplish this in the same degree.

It was many years ago that the communists announced that they planned to conquer the world. Even so there have been periods when Russia and her satellites seemed willing to cooperate with other nations. During 1955, the Russian leaders were eager to meet with President Eisenhower and the leaders of France and Great Britain. There was talk of peace and cooperation. There was a more friendly attitude than had ever before been shown by the communists.

We must hope that the communist nations led by Russia will change their aims and methods. But while communist leaders talk about peace, the great network of agents still operates throughout the world. During the summer of 1955 communist leaders met with free-world leaders at Geneva and promised to cooperate in solving the many differences between them. In 1956 the denunciation of Stalin seemed to be another indication that the communists were changing.

But the record of communist activities, in their own nations and in world affairs, remains black. It is true that restrictions on travel in Russia have been lifted to some extent; there have been changes affecting Soviet workers and farmers.

But while talking of peace at various times, the communists have continued to stir up trouble. Violations of the Korean truce continue; communist agents have attempted to cause trouble in the Middle East; communist leaders have refused to agree to a reasonable disarmament program, have visited several nations in Asia and the Middle East where they denounced America and its allies.

During the past thirty years Russia has broken almost every promise it has made. The promise to allow free elections in Eastern Europe has never been carried out. The communists have violated the Korean and Indo-China truce agreements. They have made treaties with other nations and broken them.

The magazine *U. S. News and World Report*

made a study of all the conferences in which the United States and Russia had met in order to solve world problems. Not counting the 1955 meetings at Geneva, there have been 3,400 meetings. Fifty-two agreements were reached and Russia has broken fifty of them.

The Russians promised to enter the war against Japan and they kept this promise. They kept it because it gave them a new foothold in Asia.

The latest crisis between our country and our allies and the Russians is caused by the Russian refusal to keep agreements made about Berlin. In violation of these agreements, a huge wall has been built, separating the western and eastern parts of the city. The communists have threatened to take over West Berlin. They have refused to let the German people, whether they live in East Germany or West Germany, have a free election and decide for themselves the kind of government they desire. In 1961 and 1962 Russia continually threatened war over West Berlin. These threats have made it necessary for our country to add thousands of men to our armed forces and billions of dollars to our defense budget.

CHAPTER VI

The Story of Communist China

AS WE have read about communist plans for world conquest we have frequently mentioned Russia. Communist Russia is the center of all communist planning. We may think of Russia as the father of the communist family of nations.

Among the children in this family, not all are equals. There is a big brother of special importance to the United States. Communist China, or the Chinese People's Republic, as it is called by the communists, is the only major communist nation with which we have been at war. It is the communist country which has imprisoned and tortured our soldiers and pilots.

Communist China, with over six hundred million people, is by far the largest member of the communist family. The conquest of China has been communism's greatest victory. It is important, then, to know how communism came to this country with which America had friendly relations for many years.

The communists have been in control of China since 1949. Actually there are two Chinas now. Communist China, with its capital at Peking, controls all the mainland of China. The Nationalist government, or government of Free China, controls Formosa and a few small islands near the China coast.

Even though China has been communist for only a few years, the communists have been active in that country for many years. Before the Russian communists had complete control of Russia, they were sending agents to China.

The history of China is somewhat like that of Russia. For centuries the Chinese people suffered under oppressive Emperors. A revolutionary party became very active in the early part of the twentieth century. During 1911 and 1912, the revolutionists overthrew the Manchu Dynasty which ruled at the time. But for another fifteen years there was civil war and revolution in China. The revolutionary party called the Kuomintang, or People's Party, finally achieved control of all China under the leadership of Chiang Kai-shek.

During the years of struggle in China, the

communists were at work. The Russians sent their top agents to China. At first they offered, as they have in other countries, to cooperate with the Kuomintang. But Chiang Kai-shek soon realized that cooperation with the communists was not possible. They did not want to cooperate. They wanted to dominate.

Chiang Kai-shek went to Russia to study the communist form of government. He became one of the first leaders in the modern world to understand Russian and communist aims. After visiting Moscow in 1923, Chiang wrote: "From what I have observed, the Russian communist party has absolutely no sincerity. . . . The words of the Russians are only 30 per cent dependable. Even that is an overstatement."

Unfortunately, other world leaders did not understand and did not listen to Chiang Kai-shek.

The Kuomintang under Chiang struggled against the communists for years. At one time, in the early 1930's, the communists were able to set up a government in the mountains of South China. Chiang finally drove them out of South China. The communist army marched across China and retreated into the wild mountains of Northwest China.

Even though the Chinese communist party was small, it was well organized. The communists welcomed war with Japan in 1937. They pretended to cooperate with Chiang Kai-shek in fighting the Japanese. Their army became very large and well trained. From their headquarters at Yenan, the communists conducted an unceasing propaganda program against Chiang.

When World War II ended, the communists were strong and Nationalist China was weak. China had been at war for eight years. The people were tired, they wanted peace. There was corruption in the Nationalist government. The communists promised a "new deal" if they ruled China. Unfortunately, many Americans believed communist promises. The American government tried to force Chiang Kai-shek to cooperate with the communists. There were Americans who said that the Chinese communists were not real communists. They were described as reformers who would give China good government.

After the end of World War II the Chinese communists received much aid from Russia. Discipline and morale in the communist armies were excellent. The communists began to push out of their mountain strongholds in the North-west. Gradually they defeated the tired and un-disciplined armies of Nationalist China. By late 1949, all of China was in communist control. Chiang Kai-shek and his government were driven to the island of Formosa.

In winning China, the communists won over six hundred million people and a country with rich natural resources. But they won even more than that. Many years ago Russian leaders said that "the road to Paris lies through Peking and Calcutta." This means that the communists be-lieve that Europe can be conquered by first conquering Asia. If we consider the vast popula-tions of countries like China and India, we can understand how the communists believe this. If all of Asia becomes communist, it will give the communist world enormous resources. The com-munists can threaten Africa, the Middle East, even Australia.

The Chinese communists have a powerful weapon for conquering Asia. For centuries Chinese have traveled to the other countries in Asia. Many have settled in those countries. The Chinese are good businessmen, and have gained control of business life in Malaya, in Indonesia, in Thailand. There are ten million "overseas

Chinese" now living in Southeast Asia. In the city of Singapore there are more Chinese than any other nationality.

The communists are using the overseas Chinese as a huge fifth column. Most of these Chinese are not in sympathy with the communists, but they have relatives in China. By threatening relatives, by blackmail, the Chinese communists may gain control of all the Chinese living in Southeast Asia.

Because of the Chinese communists, Asia is now filled with trouble spots. Already the Chinese communist armies have fought our soldiers in Korea. The Chinese communists helped the communists in Indo-China win half of that rich country. The Chinese communists are constantly threatening to attack Formosa. For many years Chinese communist guerrillas fought the British in the jungles of Malaya. Millions of dollars in property were destroyed during over ten years of fighting.

Communist China has become so powerful that other nations in Asia are frightened. India, Burma, and Indonesia have all tried to get along with Communist China. These countries are called *neutrals*. They do not wish to join the free world for fear of Red China. They are "fence sitters," trying to cooperate with the communist world and the free world.

The history of communism in China is much like that of Russia. Millions of people have been executed, tortured and imprisoned. The communists promised that they would give land to the peasants of China. It was for this reason that many poor Chinese farmers welcomed the communists. But instead of getting land they have to pay higher taxes than ever before. They have lost what liberties they did have.

The Chinese Communist government itself estimates that 70 per cent of the Chinese people are opposed to communism. But through a large army and police force, the communists are able to keep control. They are building a powerful army and air force. New highways and railroads are being constructed. With help from Russia, the Big Brother, Red China has become a powerful nation.

In Korea we learned that Communist China is not only powerful but also brutal. During the fighting there, 7,109 Americans were captured; 4,000 others disappeared. General Matthew Ridgeway, our commanding general during much of the Korean War, estimates that 6,000

American soldiers, airmen, and marines were murdered. Most of those who were captured and later released have told stories of terrible torture. And in 1962, nine years after the Korean truce was signed, some Americans are still being held as prisoners. The holding of prisoners is a violation of the agreements signed by the Chinese. The Chinese and North Koreans have in fact violated nearly every part of the Korean truce agreement.

The communists agreed to return all prisoners who wished to return. They agreed not to build new airfields or bring more troops into Korea after the truce. They agreed to allow neutral nations to inspect all military installations in North Korea. They have not kept any of these promises. Instead, the Chinese Reds, with Russian help, have built new airfields, have brought in hundreds of jet planes and thousands of new soldiers.

It is because of these actions on the part of Communist China that the United States still refuses to agree to admitting Red China to the United Nations. We have refused to recognize the government of Communist China. This means that we do not have an American Ambassador in that country. Instead, we recognize the government of Nationalist China on Formosa as the rightful government of China. We have pledged to defend Formosa if it is attacked by the communists.

Our relations with Communist China are the cause of great worry. Many of the nations allied with us in the free world have recognized Communist China. India, most powerful of the neutral nations, not only recognizes Red China, but often acts for her in international affairs, and in America itself there are people who believe that Red China should be recognized and should be a member of the United Nations.

Communist China, even though the junior partner in the communist world, is powerful and ambitious. The Chinese have invaded parts of India, have overrun completely the country called Tibet. In Vietnam, a country receiving American aid, communist guerrilla fighters are threatening the security of the nation. Communist China has sent thousands of agitators and teachers to Cuba, and other troublemakers have been active throughout South America.

CHAPTER VII

How America Fights Communism

SINCE the end of World War II our major problems in world affairs have been concerned with Russia and China. Yet both nations have been allied with the United States in war. Our country has a record of friendship with China going back many years. For a century it was American policy to help China become strong, to protect her from the scheming of other nations. Our history of friendship with China is well known.

Most people have forgotten that the United States has also tried to help Russia. We were the first great nation to recognize Russia when the czar was overthrown. During the 1930's American engineers helped the Russians build dams, great mills, and railroads. A Detroit engineer built Russia's largest tractor plant. Henry Ford built one of Russia's largest automobile assembly lines.

Many Americans were sympathetic with communism in Russia during this period. The suffering of the Russian people under the czars was well known, and the communists seemed to offer hope and good government. But most people soon realized that the communists were doing little more for the common people than the czars.

Since 1945, when communism became a constant threat to world peace, the United States has spent well over *two hundred billion dollars* to defend itself and other free nations against Russia and China.

It is important to understand how our country fights the menace of communism. Americans are disagreed on the best methods. There are some who believe we should spend money to help make other free nations strong. Others believe the best defense against communism is to make America the most powerful nation on earth and keep it that way.

We have tried to do both in our fight against communism. America has the largest peacetime army in history.

We have developed many new atomic weapons. We have built a long-range air force that can strike back at Russia if we are attacked.

We have established air bases all around Russia.

But at the same time we have spent billions of dollars in other ways. In our fight against communism we have used the following methods:

1.   Through gifts and loans we have spent sixty billion dollars to make other free nations strong. We call this economic aid.

2.   We have spent more billions providing other nations with arms and helping to teach their soldiers how to fight.

3.   Through the *Voice of America* and other activities of the United States Information Agency, we have carried on a world-wide propaganda program.

4.   We have banded together with other free nations in mutual security treaties.

5.   We have tried to create a peaceful world by making the United Nations strong and effective.

Let's see what has been accomplished by each of these methods.

Since the end of World War II the United States has spent approximately sixty billion dollars to provide economic aid to other nations.

The American economic assistance or foreign aid program was originally started to help na-

OUR WEAPONS FOR PEACE

A powerful modern military force

Military assistance for other
free nations

$$$ Economic aid for other free nations

Cooperation with other nations
through treaties, United Nations

The truth about democracy and
communism, told through the
Voice of America, and other media

tions get on their feet after the war. But it soon became a major defense against communism. Economically weak nations were in danger of being lost to the communists.

First known as the Marshall Plan, the program has had many names. The name of the agency administering economic aid is often changed when the Congress appropriates new funds. The present name is International Cooperation Administration, or ICA. In 1961, a special aid program for Latin America, called the Alliance for Progress, was established.

But whatever the name, the aim of economic aid or foreign assistance has been the same. We know that communism has appeal for poor peoples. The communists promise land for the landless, better wages, better housing, better clothes. If it is possible to create this better life in other ways, communism will lose it appeal.

American dollars have gone to countries all over the world. The nations of Europe have received more than twenty-five billion dollars of economic aid. Here are a few examples:

Great Britain has received nearly
    $7,000,000,000.
France has received over $5,000,000,000.

West Germany has received $3,800,000,000.
Italy has received $2,700,000,000.
Turkey has received $286,000,000.
Greece has received $1,260,000,000.

It would be difficult to find a non-communist country that has not received help from America. American money has been used to rebuild factories, to build highways, ships, and railroads. It has been used to provide farmers with tractors and other equipment.

Sometimes, in fact frequently, American aid money has been misused. Sometimes the Americans who have administered aid programs have allowed money to be wasted. But even so we must admit that through American help much of the world is prosperous today. Especially is the prosperity of Western Europe due to American help.

But is it true that American money has everywhere stopped the march of communism? France and Italy have received a total of nearly eight billion dollars. But in both countries the communist party is powerful. The government of France has been willing to make peace with the communists on almost any terms. In spite of all our help to France, she was unable to defeat the communists in Indo-China.

American dollars do not necessarily stop the communists. American aid must be understood by the people and must be honestly administered by their governments, or it will be worthless.

There are nations where American aid has been appreciated and properly used. American dollars and military assistance saved Greece at a time when communism was about to take over. The government of Turkey has made excellent use of American assistance. It has become one of the most reliable nations on the free-world side. The people of Turkey are anticommunist, they appreciate what America has done to help.

American dollars have also flowed into Asia. We have spent billions of dollars rebuilding the damage caused by the war in Korea. An army of 60,000 Americans must be kept in that country. We have helped our former enemy, Japan, so that it is now a prosperous nation. Our aid dollars have flowed in to the Republic of the Philippines and all the nations of Southeast Asia.

In the chapter on Communist China we learned that the United States still recognizes the government of Free, or Nationalist, China on Formosa. Each year approximately one hundred million dollars has been spent by the United States on that small island. Formosa is an excellent example of what American help can do to answer the promises of communism.

The Chinese Communists have always appealed to the poor peasants of Asia by promising that they shall own their own land. The so-called land reform program of the communists had great appeal until the farmers have found out that it is not all it promises to be. On Formosa, with American assistance, the Free Chinese have developed an honest land reform program.

A large proportion of Formosan farmers had never owned their land. They rented from landowners, paying up to 60 per cent of their farm yield for rent. The Formosan land reform program has forced all the big landowners to sell land to their tenants. Each farmer is able to buy his land, paying for it in installments over a ten-year period. In addition, the government of Free China has provided fertilizers, new seed varieties, insecticides. As a result of the land reform program, the farmers of Formosa own their own land, are building new homes, buying new farm equipment and raising more crops than at any time in Formosa's history.

American dollars helped make Formosa's land reform program possible. American agricultural experts have helped to make Formosan farms prosperous. Needless to say, the farmers of Formosa are not interested in communism now.

Military assistance has generally been given along with economic assistance. Here also there have been failures and successes. American military assistance saved Greece from the communists. It has helped make the Turkish army one of the best and strongest in the world. It has created in the South Korean army the largest and best-trained anti-communist force in Asia.

But American help did not keep the French from being defeated in Indo-China. Many experts do not believe that our assistance has created a reliable French army.

Military assistance has included the gift of tanks, ships, and guns. It also includes American military training missions. These are groups of American soldiers, sailors, and airmen who go to other nations and help their people to develop a modern military force. Hundreds of foreign officers have been brought to the United States to study in our military training schools.

Here are a few examples of how Americans

are training other people to fight. In Formosa a Military Assistance Advisory Group of several thousand officers and men has helped the Free Chinese create a modern army and a small jet air force. Americans have helped the Turkish army modernize. An American advisory group is assisting the government of Pakistan to establish an efficient army. Small military advisory groups are working in many of the countries of Central and South America. Altogether, American training groups are working in thirty-four countries.

In addition to trying to create prosperous conditions and efficient fighting forces, the United States has led the free world into mutual defense treaties and organizations.

The nations of Western Europe are banded together with America into the North Atlantic Treaty Organization, called NATO. NATO is working to create an army, well trained and supplied, able to fight back immediately if Europe is attacked by Russia. Through NATO and as a result of other treaties, the United States has established air bases in England, in Europe, North Africa and even in the arctic regions.

In Asia there is an organization called

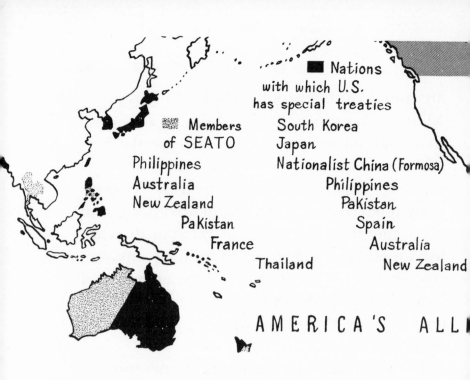

Members of SEATO
Philippines
Australia
New Zealand
Pakistan
France
Thailand

■ **Nations with which U.S. has special treaties**
South Korea
Japan
Nationalist China (Formosa)
Philippines
Pakistan
Spain
Australia
New Zealand

AMERICA'S ALL

SEATO, which means the Southeast Asia Treaty Organization, in which the United States has joined with a number of nations in a mutual defense organization. In addition, our nation has mutual assistance treaties with Nationalist China on Formosa, with the Republic of South Korea and the Republic of the Philippines. In Japan we are helping to create a small army and air force for the defense of this country which was our enemy not too long ago.

In trying to create a powerful free world, the United States has given aid to Communist Poland and Yugoslavia. The communist leaders of Yugo-

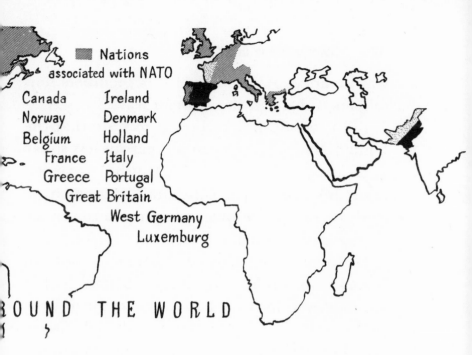

Nations associated with NATO

Canada   Ireland
Norway   Denmark
Belgium   Holland
France   Italy
Greece   Portugal
Great Britain
West Germany
Luxemburg

slavia have broken away from Russia. This country has received over one billion dollars to help create better economic conditions. However, on most questions Yugoslavia still sides with the other communist nations.

The United States is a member of the United Nations. All of the major communist countries except China are also members. The free-world nations have tried to work for peace through the UN. There they have been able to debate world problems with communist members. The UN branded North Korea and Communist China as aggressor nations when South Korea was invaded. A number of UN members sent soldiers to help in the Korean war.

But it would not be honest to state that the United Nations has been a great success so far in creating a peaceful world. Russia has vetoed many measures. The communist nations have used the UN for propaganda purposes, even for spying and espionage.

However, the United Nations action in Korea was important. Never before had a group of nations thus banded together to fight an aggressor in a distant land. Although American and South Korean soldiers did most of the fighting, a dozen other nations sent troops. Turkish, Greek, Dutch, French, British, and Canadian soldiers were among those who fought with Americans under the United Nations command. The soldiers of the United Nations fought bravely. Unfortunately many UN members did not send help. Russia, although a member, helped the communist aggressors. In spite of the fact that the communists have violated the Korean truce agreement, the United Nations has not taken action.

The UN has also failed to live up to a pledge to help rebuild South Korea. After the fighting ended, it was agreed that since the Korean War was a United Nations war, the UN members should help rebuild the country. Only a few UN countries have been able to help.

Unless people want to be free, no amount of help can keep them free. In order to understand and want freedom, people everywhere need to understand communism. Since the United States has become the free-world leader, people need also to understand the United States and its aims. Propaganda has therefore become a cold war weapon.

Through the Voice of America, and other programs of the United States Information Agency, America has spent from $75,000,000 to $100,000,000 each year for the past ten years, trying to tell its story to the rest of the world.

The Voice of America broadcasts in many languages, telling people about America and about our way of life. The United States Information Agency, of which the Voice of America is a part, has offices all over the world. It maintains libraries where people can read about America. Foreign students are brought to the United States to study. Newspapers are published, motion pictures are sent into faraway places.

But the story of American propaganda is like that of economic aid. There have been successes and also failures. Unfortunately, there are very few radios in many countries. In communist countries it is illegal to listen to the Voice of America. People can be sent to slave labor camps for tuning in an American radio station.

Very few people in the countries of Asia or Latin America can read English. They do not learn much from the fine books which are printed in English and displayed in libraries in their countries. Too often the Voice of America and the Information Offices have told about the wonders of life in America. The poor people of the world see pictures of beautiful American homes and farms. They are told that nearly all Americans own automobiles. They know that such prosperity will be impossible for them. Instead of helping make people want to stay free, this propaganda often merely makes them dissatisfied.

But the Voice of America has reached some people, we know. It has given hope to people shut off from news of the outside world. It has given some people courage to escape from communist countries. The American propaganda program has been neither all good nor all bad. It has sometimes helped people understand America better.

In another chapter of this book we learned that one of the greatest weapons used by the communists is their party, with its members scattered all over the world. In America's fight against communism we must not only try to strengthen other free nations. We must also be on guard against the communists in America.

A few years ago there were 100,000 Communist Party members in America. Now there are between 23,000 and 25,000. There are several reasons why the Communist Party has lost members. During the past ten years many party members have begun to understand communism and have left the party. In 1954, Congress passed the Butler-Humphrey Act. The Communist Party is now no longer a legal political party. Anyone who belongs to it, and who openly advocates the overthrow of our government can be arrested and prosecuted. Already a number of top communists have been imprisoned. Through the work of Congressional committees and the FBI, most of the subversive employees of the government have been removed.

The FBI keeps a close watch on all known communists. In case of war the communists could be quickly arrested.

Although many members of the Communist Party in the United States have been forced to go underground, the party is still dangerous. For every party member, there are many people called "fellow travelers," or men and women who, although not Communist Party members, still follow the communist line.

It is more difficult to fight communism in America than in many other countries, for the American way of life guarantees freedom of expression. American officials cannot arrest all people who express communist views. The Smith Act, passed in 1940, makes it possible to arrest people who knowingly advocate overthrow of our government by force. But a newspaper writer or a radio commentator may express views which are much the same as the communist line, so long as he does not urge overthrow of the government. For example, though many Americans believe that we should never recognize Communist China, other Americans advocate that Communist China be recognized and be immediately admitted to the United Nations. Of course the communists want these same things.

But this does not mean that Americans who hold the same views should be arrested.

America's greatest defense against communism is education. If everyone understands communism we have nothing to fear. It is largely because many of us did not understand communist aims that so much of the world is under communist rule now.

CHAPTER VIII

What of the Future?

We NOW have a good idea of what communism is, what it stands for and how it operates. The world, part communist, part free, is not healthy. We must admit that in some parts of the world some people have benefited because of communism. We must admit that under communist rule, highways, factories, irrigation systems have been built where none existed. The communists have made great scientific advances, have established powerful military forces.

But whatever good things have come of communism have been counterbalanced by the loss of liberties and the tyranny of communist rule. Furthermore, as long as world conquest is a communist aim, we cannot ignore the communist world because communism threatens the liberty of people everywhere.

The enemy we face does not play by any rules.

He is ruthless and scheming, makes promises that are not kept. Broken communist promises have changed the lives of millions of people, have even changed the maps of the world. Because of communism the United States was involved in the Korean War. Because of communism the United States must continue to spend billions of dollars for defense.

What is the solution of this problem, of the rivalry between the free world led by America and the communist world led by Russia? Different people have different ideas. We might condense these into three general solutions:

1. There are people who believe that the only solution to the communist problem is war between the United States and the communist nations. Some Americans have even advocated "preventive war." By this is meant a war which America itself would start, striking at Russia and Communist China before these nations become so strong they will strike at us.

2. Many people, not only in America, but all over the world, believe that "coexistence" is the only solution. The free world would mind its business while the communist nations mind theirs. Trade between the free and communist worlds would be increased. In other words, both

sides would avoid conflict, would adopt a "live and let live" policy.

3. Some experts believe that the problem of communism will be solved from within, by the millions of people who live in communist-ruled Nations. We know that most of these people are unhappy. It is thought that in time people will rebel, will overthrow their communist masters. Already there have been serious rebellions in the communist world. If communist rule continues to be brutal, if the communist peoples continue to be oppressed, it is hoped that they will strike back and thus bring peace and security to the world.

We shall not advocate any of these solutions. Instead, let's look at some of the problems connected with each.

For instance, there is little likelihood our country would ever start a war, is there? We are not that type of people. And thoughtful people everywhere realize that a war, no matter who started it, might wreck the whole world. Perhaps no one would really win such a war. The United States and Russia both have atomic weapons. Both are powerful nations. While it is almost certain that we would defeat the communists, there might not be much left of our country when the war was completed.

Coexistence may be the only solution to the communist problem. But it is an expensive and somewhat dangerous policy. Many people advocate increased trade with the communist nations as a part of coexistence. It is thought that this would reduce tension. But by establishing more trade we would be making communism stronger. Most of the communist nations have serious economic problems. They need food and manufactured goods they cannot themselves produce. Increased trade would make the communist countries stronger and more able to fulfill their plans for world conquest.

These plans have not yet changed. The network of communist spies and agents is still active all over the world. A policy of coexistence will mean that the free world must continue to be alert, must spend much money on arms. The United States must continue to help other nations, as well as to keep itself strong. Coexistence will cost a great deal of money unless the communists agree to disarmament, unless they also agree to disband their network of agents.

It is certainly to be hoped that the peoples of

the communist nations will rebel. That would be the best solution—for the people who have suffered most to strike back and win their freedom. In 1953 there was a serious rebellion in East Germany.

In 1956 there were days of rioting in Poland where workers demonstrated against the communist government. And in Hungary there was a revolution which threatened to free the nation from communist rule. It was necessary to bring in thousands of Russian troops before the Hungarian revolt could be crushed.

The Chinese communists admit that they too have had trouble with rebellious citizens. And even though completely overrun by the Chinese army, the people of Tibet have continued to fight back.

But we must admit that the military and police control in communist-ruled nations is so strong that the chances of successful revolution are not good. If revolutions are to be successful, people will have to receive outside help. The only place effective help can come from is the United States. Yet, if we agree to a policy of coexistence, we cannot very well help people to fight their masters. The Russians certainly would object if we supplied arms to the people of Rumania, Poland, and Hungary.

So you can see that there is no easy solution. But that does not mean there is nothing we can do. There is still much that we as a people and as individuals can do to keep ourselves strong and free.

First we must understand what communism is, and that is the purpose of this book. Fifteen years ago most of the world did not understand the aims of communism. The communists cannot achieve success easily if people understand their aims and methods.

America has always been the symbol of hope to millions of people. That is something to be proud of. Within the limits of our abilities we must continue to be willing to help others who wish to remain free. This does not mean that we can wastefully give billions of dollars to other countries. It has always been the hope of the communists that the United States would destroy itself. It has been communist policy to make our government spend billions of dollars in the hope that in time we would become bankrupt as a nation and as a people.

We must not give up our hope that the United Nations may pave the way to real peace. The UN can be criticized for many failures. But it still offers hope. Through the UN the free nations can still work together. Through the UN people can be educated to the aims of communism.

The story of American aims and the democratic way of life must continue to be told to other people. This too, does not mean that we should waste money. But propaganda must continue to be a weapon. Combined with sensible aid to other nations, propaganda can help make people want to remain free. We can make new friends and keep old friends.

Of course we must always keep strong. This will mean that for many years it may be necessary to maintain a large army, navy, and air force. It will mean that military life will be experienced by thousands of young men. It will never be safe for the United States to let down its guard until communism is gone or until the communists show clearly by deeds that they have changed their aims.

Above all, we must not be ashamed of our way of life. It is much better than anything the communists have to offer. Remember that communism got its start because so many of Europe's people were oppressed. To a considerable degree the same conditions existed in America. But we have gone far to solve our social and economic problems *without communism*. American workers and farmers live better, have more security, more leisure time, and above all, more freedom than most people in the world.

This American way of life did not just happen. It has been accomplished by the very methods the communist world denounces, by what we call the free-enterprise system. It has been accomplished without tyranny and loss of freedom. The best way for America to remain free and strong is to preserve the way of life and government that has made us the most powerful nation in world history.

We must admit that our country is not perfect. There are problems that have not been solved, groups of people who do not enjoy as full a life as they should. But even with our problems and failures, we have developed a way of life that is envied by the rest of the world. There is nothing any of us can do more important than to remember this and by the practice of intelligent good citizenship make our country even better.

Good citizenship in this cold-war world also requires knowledge. In 1955 our Department of Defense established a committee to study communist brainwashing methods, to discover why some American war prisoners denounced their country and chose communism. In its report the committee stated that many of the American soldiers knew so little about the United States and its ideals and traditions that they could not even answer arguments in favor of communism. They could not fight communist arguments because they knew so little about their America.

As the report says: "At home the soldiers thought of politics as dry editorials and uninteresting speeches, dull as ditchwater." Many times the Chinese Communist and Korean Communist instructors knew more about American history and politics than the American soldiers did.

We must first of all understand that we are in a period of war. This war may last for many years; and in order to win, it may be necessary for Americans to give up some things and to sacrifice.

If our nation and the other free nations are to remain free, we must not be afraid, and we must be willing to fight if this becomes necessary. In England there are people so opposed to war that they are willing for the western nations to disarm in the hope that Russia will then become more peaceful. These people have a saying, "Better be red than dead."

But if we and our children are to remain free, it may be necessary to change this saying to, "We'd rather be dead than red." We know what life under communism has meant for millions of people; we must understand what it would mean to us. We know now that the rulers of the communist world do not keep agreements, that they cannot be trusted and that it is a communist boast that all the world will some day be under communist rule.

Although talking about peace, Russia and her allies have increased their intrigues all over the world. Every effort has been made to disrupt the United Nations and to make it ineffective. UN efforts to bring peace to the Congo have been attacked. Russian and Chinese agitators have stirred up trouble in other newly independent nations of Africa and Asia.

Cuba, our next-door neighbor in the Caribbean, has become a communist-controlled nation. Communist agents are also active in other countries of Central and South America. Laos in Southeast Asia has been overrun by communist guerrillas who receive aid and training from Russia and China. Nearby Vietnam, an American ally, is seriously threatened. And, as we have said, Russia has threatened to attack unless we agree to communist demands about West Berlin and Germany.

During the past few years the Russians have developed powerful atomic weapons. They have rockets capable of reaching any part of our country. They have threatened to use their atomic weapons against us, should we fail to agree to communist demands. We must realize that Russia has become a powerful nation, second only to the United States in its strength. However, we cannot hope to survive if we become afraid, and we must know more about and appreciate our way of life.

The American way of life is not dull; our history is exciting. Ours is a thrilling story of a great experiment that has succeeded. This success has given hope to millions of people all over the world. The American Constitution is the most copied document of its kind in the world. Every American must know and understand the story of our country. We must also know and study the history of communism, its aims and its methods. In so doing, we not only can keep ourselves free but can also give faith and hope to those who are not free or to those who are wavering in their faith in democracy.

We should always remember the words of President Kennedy, who has said that it will not be necessary for Americans to be "either dead or red."

Index